To

G000077172

2020
xx

Slothology

Don't Hurry. Be Happy.

ISBN: 978-1-912511-33-4

Created by Christina Rose
Contributors: Nataly Popovych, Shutterstock

DON'T hurry
DO everything in a
peaceful and calm Spirit

Note to Self - relax

Sometimes it's
absolutely necessary to
shut down, kick back
and do nothing

calm is a superpower

peace begins with
a smile

Being busy is seriously
overrated. Slow down
and relax

Let your mind and heart rest for a while

Don't stress over what
you can't control
Slow down and focus
on the positive

Pick your own pace
and your own path
we must all relax
and recharge

your future depends
on your dreams
so go to sleep

sleep is the best
meditation

If you are
always racing
to the next moment
what happens to the
one you're in?

we would do well
to slow down a little,
focus on the significant
and truly see the things
that matter most

you have enough
you do enough
you ARE enough... chill

A well spent day brings happy sleep

whatever happens
happens.
Don't worry
Don't hurry. Be happy

slowing down allows us
to realise that life
is about progress
not perfection

Slow down
and everything
you are chasing
will come around
and catch you

Be grateful
Slow down
ENjoy life

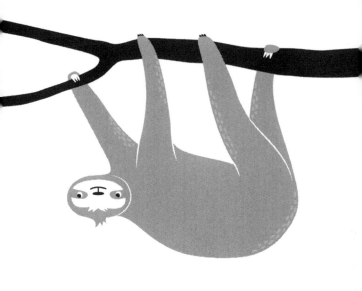

Taking time to do
nothing often brings
everything into
perspective

Let's stop telling each other how busy we are

The body benefits from
movement
The mind benefits from
stillness

Each person deserves
a day away in which
no problems are
confronted and no
solutions searched for

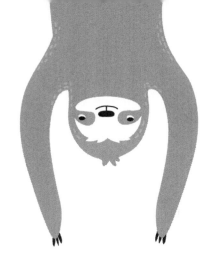

Sometimes the most urgent and vital thing you can possibly do is to take a complete rest

Take time to notice
the things that other
people are overlooking

Good vibes only
Take it as it comes

Sometimes all you need
to do is slow down
and relax

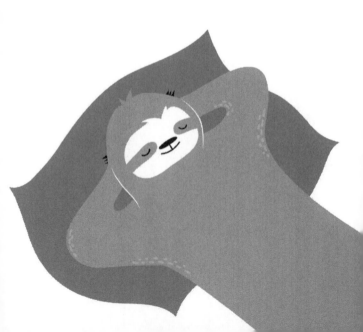

Life's a journey not a
race. Slow down, enjoy
the view, relax
and let it happen

The day you stop racing
is the day you win
the race

Sometimes the most productive thing you can do is slow down

calm down and slow
down
Everything will be
okay

Be peaceful
Be happy
Be whole

slowing down is
sometimes the best way
to speed up

Slow down
Rushing means you miss
what's right here

Take a deep breath
It's not a race

A beautiful day begins
with a beautiful mind
Enjoy your day
and relax

Give yourself permission
to slow down

Take it easy
Everything happens
when the time is right

keep calm, slow down
and focus
on the positive

you create your own
calm by how you live
your life

Rest until you feel like playing. Play until you feel like resting. Never do anything else.

DON'T STRESS
DO YOUR BEST
FORGET THE REST

Everyday is a second chance to slow down and get it right

when you take your
time great things
happen

Remain calm
peace equals power

All that is important
comes in quietness
and waiting

DON'T WORRY
DON'T hurry
Trust the process

you can do anything
but not everything

DON'T rush Something
that you want to last
forever

Life is much easier
when you chill out

INVEST IN REST

set peace of mind
as your highest goal

strength
is how calmly
you face life

when in doubt...
chill out

How beautiful it is
to do nothing and then
rest afterward

Stop focusing on how
stressed you are
and remember
how blessed you are

Be gentle with yourself
you're doing the best
you can

Life goes by fast
Slow down and enjoy it

Learn to calm the winds of your mind

Let everything
happen naturally
Don't force it

Take time to do what
makes you happy

Go where you feel most at peace

Go with the flow and take it easy